Lancashire

Ron Freethy

COUNTRYSIDE BOOKS
NEWBURY BERKSHIRE

First Published 2007
© Ron Freethy, 2007

COUNTRYSIDE BOOKS
3 Catherine Road
Newbury, Berkshire

To view our complete range of books,
please visit us at
www.countrysidebooks.co.uk

ISBN 978 1 84674 019 0

Photographs by the author
Cover picture showing the River Hodder in Bowland
supplied by Bill Meadows

Designed by Peter Davies, Nautilus Design
Produced through MRM Associates Ltd, Reading
Printed by Cambridge University Press

Contents

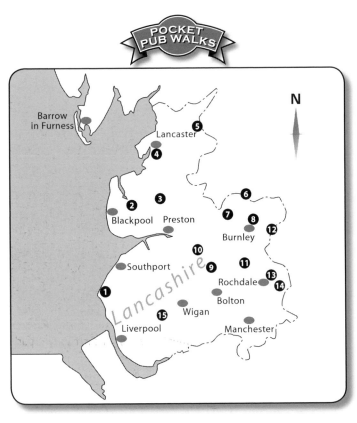

Area map showing location of the walks

Introduction

I love walking in Lancashire because the county is so varied. It has an extensive coastline, sweeping moorlands, lush fields, beautiful woodland, canals and reservoirs, as well as rivers of interest to naturalists and anglers. The walks in this book reflect that diversity, from the wonderful views to be enjoyed from Ashurst Beacon or towards Pendle Hill, to woodland strolls on the Formby Dunes and along the estuary of the River Wyre. Every walk reveals something of historic interest or fascinating wildlife.

My selection of only fifteen walks had to be made from many of my favourite routes which I have explored over the last 40 years. I have had the pleasant company of one wife, one son, one grandson and a succession of three black Labradors. My choice was greatly influenced by these companions.

Much of the scenery has changed surprisingly little over time but the rivers of the county are now much cleaner, as is the quality of the air. The pubs have also changed and now offer excellent refreshments, including some local ales. Tea, coffee, soft drinks and sandwiches are all available, in addition to menus offering a mouth-watering mixture of local and worldwide dishes. All the walks, which vary in length from 1½ to 6 miles, are circular and the directions include details of an excellent pub, either at the start or finish of the stroll or along the route, with telephone numbers so that you can check opening times and food availability. Parking directions are given, but if you want to leave your car in the car park of the inn while you walk, it is only courteous to ask the permission of the landlord first. The relevant Ordnance Survey map is listed for each walk. There is also a note on places of interest nearby so that you can make a day of it if you wish.

I hope all who love gentle walks in these wonderfully varied areas will enjoy my routes and that families and canine companions will have lots to appreciate.

Ron Freeay

Publisher's Note

We hope that you obtain considerable enjoyment from this book; great care has been taken in its preparation. However, changes of landlord and actual closures are sadly not uncommon. Likewise, although at the time of publication all routes followed public rights of way or permitted paths, diversion orders can be made and permissions withdrawn.

We cannot, of course, be held responsible for such diversion orders and any inaccuracies in the text which result from these or any other changes to the routes nor any damage which might result from walkers trespassing on private property. We are anxious though that all details covering the walks and pubs are kept up to date and would therefore welcome information from readers which would be relevant to future editions.

The simple sketch maps that accompany the walks in this book are based on notes made by the author whilst checking out the routes on the ground. However, for the benefit of a proper map, we do recommend that you purchase the relevant Ordnance Survey sheet covering your walk. The Ordnance Survey maps are widely available, especially through booksellers and local newsagents.

1 Formby Dunes

The Freshfield

Here, set amidst spectacular coastal scenery and one of the highlights of this walk through sand dunes and woodland, is an area regarded as one of the best places in England to watch rare red squirrels. They do not hibernate and can be seen at their best during winter, when they come close to those who offer them food, which can be purchased at the entrance to the car park. In summer the sand dune flowers are spectacular and equally colourful are some of the autumn fungi. In the autumn and spring the bird migratory movements

Distance 2½ miles.

OS Explorer 285 Southport and Chorley. GR 272083.

A level walk for all seasons, with plenty of sheltered spots from which to enjoy seaside views.

Starting Point The National Trust fee paying car park at Freshfield on Formby Dunes.

How to get there On the A565, which links Southport and Liverpool, turn off at a roundabout at Formby that carries National Trust brown signs indicating Freshfield and the Dunes. Cross the level crossing over the railway and follow the National Trust signs along Victoria Road, which is a cul-de-sac. Follow the narrow track to a large hardstanding parking area set amidst trees and extensive sand dunes.

are often worth travelling miles to see. Picnic areas abound and dogs are even welcome in the squirrel area but obviously they should be kept on a lead.

THE PUB The **Freshfield**, approximately 400 yards from the railway station, is a traditional family pub which welcomes walkers. There are often bargain offers on the varied menu but my favourite is the Full Monty Breakfast which is served all day and which is a joy at the conclusion of the walk. There is a snack 'n' share option which includes chicken and mushroom nachos and garlic bread. The range of beers is extensive but drivers are ensured of good tea and coffee. The delicious desserts include sticky toffee pudding, which is an ideal warmer on a cold day.

☎ *01704 874871*

Formby Dunes Walk 1

1 From the car park, face the sea and look for a footpath to the right. Follow this undulating track through the dunes.

Efforts have been made to stabilise the sand by planting marram grass and especially buckthorn. In the autumn and winter the orange berries of buckthorn provide food for birds, especially migrating redwing and fieldfare. The obvious path then bears left towards the shore and a golf course is away to the right. Here is the perfect habitat for breeding birds such as stonechat, meadow pipit and skylark.

2 The path ascends gently to a viewing platform from where you will see a picnic site.

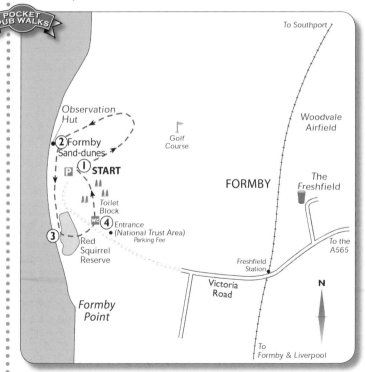

Walking through the dunes.

This viewing platform is an ideal point from which to watch birds, especially when the wind is blowing from the sea. Here, a winter watch will reveal thousands of birds such as knot and dunlin, but including a number of rare species. The coastal scenery should be enjoyed and never rushed. When you are ready, turn left and inland away from the viewing platform. Take time at the picnic site to look around the woodland area, especially in the autumn when the fungi can be of great interest. Here grows the fly agaric, which is shining red with white blotches on it. This species delighted the artist in Beatrix Potter, who did not begin life as a writer of children's stories. She was an expert on fungi, worked for the Natural History Museum in London and illustrated books on the subject. Fly agaric is poisonous and at one time it was used if flies became troublesome in a sickroom. It was heated up with milk and a saucer was placed in the bedroom of a sick person; the mixture attracted the flies and the poison killed them.

3 From the picnic site, turn left onto what has become known as the **Squirrel Walk**.

This area consists of a large stand of Scots pine which is the perfect habitat for the red squirrel. Unlike the American grey squirrel, which was introduced into Britain in the 1870s, the red squirrel is native and has been here since the end of the Ice Ages. Its scientific name is Sciurus vulgaris, the latter word meaning common. At one time the red squirrel was regarded as a pest. Large-scale forest clearance has been regarded as the main reason for its decline but the worry these days is the presence of a deadly virus which only affects this one species and is a real threat. Grey squirrels carry the disease but are not themselves affected by it. The red squirrel is much smaller and more delicate than the more aggressive American grey, which usually has two litters of young per year whilst the red almost always has only one.

Bear left around the **Squirrel Walk** and approach the entrance road.

4 At the road is a toilet block and there is often an ice cream van parked nearby. From the block, an obvious footpath descends very gently to the left and through an extensive area of mixed woodlands.

This is the preserve of the resident birds, including the shy great spotted woodpecker, whilst the cheeky magpies and jays are experts at stealing the food meant for the squirrels.

This woodland stroll after about ½ mile leads back to the **car park** and the starting point.

Places of interest nearby

Southport, a few miles north on the A565, is a well-appointed seaside town which suits modern visitors, especially those who want to enjoy varied shopping, splendid Edwardian architecture and the gentle ambience of the resort.

Churchtown is the ancient settlement in the Southport area and has a splendid church, an impressive old hall and colourful botanic gardens, all close to the Ribble estuary. There are lots of thatched cottages and traditional teashops.

2 Skippool

The River Wyre Hotel

This walk follows the estuary of the River Wyre, starting from the ancient seaport of Skippool and passing Cockle Hall before returning via the Wyreside Ecology Centre. Whatever the time of year, the views on this stroll are spectacular, with boats on the river adding to the colourful scene. The birdlife is varied at high or low tide and you may see shelduck, curlew, redshank and black-tailed godwit. In the summer botanists delight in the flowers, including thrift, sea purslane, bird's foot trefoil, elder and sea centaury.

Distance 4 miles.

OS Explorer 286 Blackpool and Preston, 296 Lancaster, Morecambe and Fleetwood. GR 356410.

A level walk along the estuary of the River Wyre. Tide timetables are for sale at the Ecology Centre (☎ 01253 857890) but this walk is safe whatever the state of the tide.

Starting Point The large free car park at Skippool.

How to get there From the A585 Blackpool to Fleetwood road, approach a large roundabout with the River Wyre Hotel at the crossroads. A minor road (B5412) is signed from the roundabout to Skippool Creek and Stanah. After less than 300 yards turn sharp right along a narrow road to Skippool. In about 400 yards there is a free car park on the left.

THE PUB

The **River Wyre Hotel**, built in the mid-19th century, looks much older and resembles a half-timbered manor house. Seen from Skippool Creek it looks a real treat. The interior is friendly and spaciously comfortable. The menu is varied and the establishment is very busy at the weekend when the famous Sunday roasts are served. Freshly cut sandwiches and a wide variety of coffees are also on offer. I loved the salt beef with gherkins and English mustard, and the fish dishes include salmon, hake and swordfish, which are all excellent value. The minted lamb shank and chargrilled calves' liver and bacon are also popular.

☎ 01253 883791

Lancashire

1. From the car park at **Skippool**, turn left and follow the wide track alongside the **River Wyre**, with the boats and their associated wooden jetties providing both colour and interest.

   It is said that a couple of small boats from Skippool took part in the evacuation of Dunkirk in 1940. Skippool was once a busy port and from 1700 small sailing ships from the Baltic and West Indies imported timber, wine, rum, sugar and tobacco. Look on the opposite side of the estuary to see the modern Shard Bridge, which replaced an old toll bridge and the port of Wardley's Creek. In the mid-18th century the dual ports of Wardley's Creek and Skippool were governed from Poulton-le-Fylde and together handled more cargo than Liverpool. When Fleetwood was built in 1840 these two minor Wyreside ports declined and are now set in a haunting time warp.

Skippool Creek.

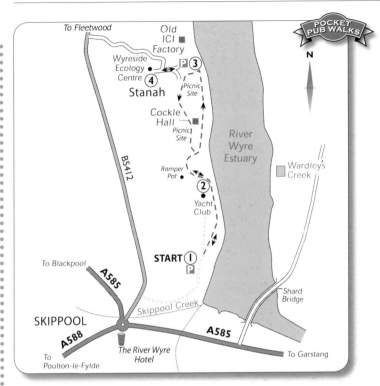

2 Continue past the often busy **Yacht Club** towards **Ramper Pot**.

There are splendid views over the estuary from Ramper Pot, which is a sheltered and attractive hollow. In the summer, this is the place to look out for butterflies such as red admirals, painted ladies and orange tips.

The route then passes through the **Cockle Hall** picnic site.

Cockle Hall was not so much a hall as a cottage, once the base for a ferry crossing over the river, which operated until the 1930s. Travellers had to summon the ferryman by waving to him, sometimes from the opposite bank. Look out for the damson trees originally planted by the ferryman's family.

Continue along the obvious path, passing a small picnic site on the left.

3 Bear left away from the water. Pass through a large free car park, with lots of seats located at panaromic viewing points. Continue and reach the **Wyreside Ecology Centre** at **Stanah**.

The Ecology Centre has operated since 1989 and is overlooked by the old ICI factory at Thornton. Salt has been produced in the area since 1890 and its derivatives were a vital commodity during two world wars and beyond. The centre and toilets are open daily.

4 From the **Ecology Centre**, return along the outward route to the picnic site. At the car park the path forks. Take the right fork and pass through a gate. Follow the footpath to the left. This passes alongside a hedge with lots of pleasantly located seats. It leads back to **Ramper Pot**. From this point follow your outward route to return to the car park at **Skippool**.

Places of interest nearby

The **Fleetwood Museum** at nearby Fleetwood is a compact museum describing the history and natural history of the port. There are details and artefacts relating to the fishing and salt industries and also extensive displays covering the wildlife of the area. The museum includes a bookshop and a small café.
☎ *01253 876621*

Freeport is an extensive shopping centre close to the Fisherman's Friend factory which is world famous because of its lozenges.

The **Fleetwood market** is one of the largest and best in the whole of Northern England, attracting people from far and wide in response to the bargains which are always on offer.
☎ *01253 771651*

3 Great Eccleston

The Cartford Hotel

This is a fascinating stroll through history and allows time to explore the ancient settlement of Great Eccleston, with its market square lined with shops, pubs and restaurants. Naturalists and lovers of lush countryside will revel in this walk, which concludes by ascending to the sweeping meander of the lovely River Wyre, passing along riverside banks that are the haunt of the resident heron and kingfisher. Sandmartins and common sandpipers are summer visitors. This is the English countryside at its very best.

THE PUB The **Cartford Hotel** is unique in Lancashire in that there is a small brewery attached to it. The name 'Cart Ford' indicates a shallow ford and the hostelry was used as a stopping point by travellers using the ancient crossing. When the turnpike road

Distance 2½ miles.

OS Explorer 286 Blackpool and Preston. **OL** 41 Forest of Bowland and Ribblesdale. GR 424407.

A gentle undulating walk across lush fields.

Starting Point The Cartford Hotel, near Cartford toll bridge.

How to get there On the A586 approaching Great Eccleston from the east, look out for a sign on the opposite side indicating Cartford Toll Bridge and Pilling. Follow the narrow, winding but well-signed road to Cartford. It is about ½ mile to the pub. There is some street parking close to the toll bridge and the Cartford Hotel has a large car park at the rear. Visitors using the hotel should ask at the bar if wanting to leave their car whilst they walk.

was built in the late 18th century, a toll bridge replaced the ford and has operated ever since. The Cartford Hotel retains all its traditional atmosphere with small, cosy rooms and beams being a feature. The menu is varied and includes vegetarian options, while the meat come. from a local butcher and the fish choice is wide. There is an imaginative children's menu and the favourite of many adults is lamb's liver and onions served with creamy mashed potatoes. The next-door Hart Brewery's hand-pumped ales are on sale and there is also a good range of other beers, but tea and coffee are available, too. If you fancy an extra tot of an unusual spirit, you may get a glimpse of the ghost of a traveller who died at the inn in the 19th century.

☎ *01995 670166*

Either now or at the end of the walk, take time to look at the old toll bridge. Drivers pay a modest toll but pedestrians can cross free of charge and from the bridge there are splendid views of the River Wyre.

1 To begin the walk, at the rear of the **Cartford Hotel** look out for a ladder stile close to the river. The footpath sweeps away from the river to the left. This leads to a hedged path, which gradually ascends to meet the **A586**.

2 Cross the **A586** and continue along a footpath leading to the well-named **Back Lane** in **Great Eccleston**. Pass through rows

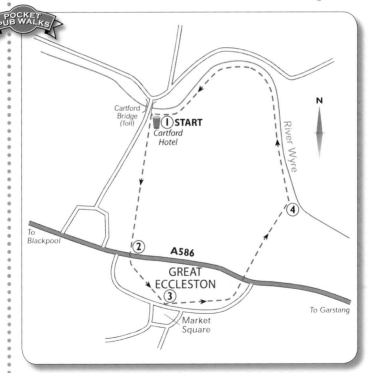

The toll bridge.

of 17th- and 18th-century cottages and then reach the backyards of buildings looking out onto the main street. Turn right to reach the market square.

In the Domesday Book the village was referred to as 'Eglestun', which means 'the place of the church'. An ancient (perhaps Saxon) church has long vanished and the present St Anne's dates to 1723 and was substantially enlarged in the 19th century. Farming has always been vital to the village and the so-called 'Great Ecc' Show held in the late summer is well supported. Across the main square the Black Bull and the White Bull face each other and offer excellent bar snacks. Both were busy with travellers during the 19th century before the A586 bypass was built; Great Eccleston was then on the main coaching route linking Lancaster with the Fylde.

3 Follow the main street until it meets the **A586**. Cross this, turn left and after a few yards pass through a gateway very close to a bus shelter. This leads to a substantial hedgerow close to a water treatment works. Here there is a stile. Cross this and follow a well-worn and obvious path which ascends gently towards the **River Wyre**.

4 At the **Wyre** embankment bear left and look to the east for views of the **Trough of Bowland**. Turn left and cross three stiles, walking close to a row of buildings. Ignore the substantial footbridge over the **Wyre** to the right. The route swings left along the riverbank and in around 1 mile returns to the toll bridge and the **Cartford Hotel** where you began.

Places of interest nearby

Farmer Parr's Animal World, situated at Rossall Lane, on the Fleetwood road, is an excellent amenity, with a nature trail, a display of farm animals and a large museum devoted to agriculture and industry of the Fylde.
☎ *01253 8744389*

Marsh Mill Village at Thornton-Cleveleys, with shops, café and a pub, is focused on Marsh Mill, also known as the Red Mill. This grain mill was built in 1794 and has been sensitively restored. Guided tours are on offer.
☎ *01253 860765*

The Stork Hotel

Splendid views of the sea and an estuary so rich in natural history that birdwatchers and botanists travel miles to enjoy the area, enhance this relaxing stroll. It follows an old railway line across a viaduct over the River Conder and onwards to an attractive marina and canal towpath. New, well laid out and signed footpaths and picnic areas have been developed and landscaped around Glasson Dock, itself a fascinating small port.

THE PUB Once a substantial farmhouse, the **Stork** has been a hotel since 1660. A board inside the bar lists the landlords since that time, resembling that of a church with its list of vicars! It has been the Stork since the 1850s but was once named the Cocks and was famous for cock fighting. Later it was called the Hamilton Arms after the duke of that name who once owned the land hereabouts.

The hotel offers bar snacks and a restaurant located in what was once the stable block. The food is varied but has a real local flavour to it. Don't miss the Morecambe Bay shrimps or the smoked haddock or salmon which have been cured about a mile away at the Glasson Dock Smokery. There are also locally produced sausages and steak and kidney suet puddings. Hand-pulled ales are also a feature and walkers and dogs are welcome. The choice of coffees and sandwiches is equally wide.

☎ 01524 751234

Distance 3 miles.

OS Explorer 296 Lancaster, Morecambe and Fleetwood.
OS OL 41 Forest of Bowland and Ribblesdale. GR 458561

A gentle and level walk.

Starting Point Conder Green picnic site close to the Stork Hotel.

How to get there From the A588 going north towards Lancaster, pass the turning to Glasson and watch out on the left for the Stork Hotel. Turn left and follow a track to the large free car park at Conder Green.

Lancashire

1 Start at the **Conder Green car park**.

This is on the site of the old station of the London and North Western Railway that was a single-line track completed in 1883 and which ran from Glasson Dock to Lancaster via Conder Green. The line closed to passenger traffic in 1930 and to goods traffic in 1964. Since then it has served as a linear nature reserve.

From the car park head off towards **Glasson** which is clearly signed and, in less than 200 yards, turn right and cross the viaduct over the **River Conder**, which is a pretty little tributary of the **Lune**.

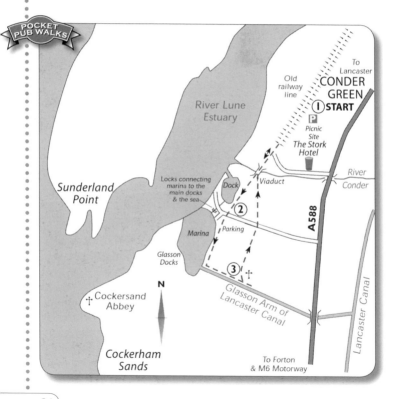

Glasson Dock.

This is the place to see seabirds and waders such as lapwing, curlew and oystercatchers. It is an excellent place to watch birds in winter or during the spring and autumn migrations. This is part of the Lancashire Coastal Footpath.

Follow the obvious path and bear right along the line of seats and the extensive picnic area. Turn left (there are public toilets on the right).

2 Cross the minor road to the **Glasson** pay and display car park.

From here you can explore the village, the canal locks, the historic pubs and, away to the right, the fish smokehouse and shop. Glasson Dock was purpose-built to replace Lancaster docks when, in the early 19th century, larger vessels were being built and the River Lune was silting up. The deep water dock with stone jetties was built in order to rival Liverpool. The ambitious scheme failed but Glasson is still a fascinating and functional small port.

Bear left, leaving the marina on the right. Continue until you reach the Glasson Branch of the Lancaster Canal. The dock and canal were completed in the early 1800s and they are wonderful places to watch boats and talk to friendly boating people.

Stroll along the canal footpath till you reach the small **church of All Saints**.

As you approach the church, built at the same time as the canal, look out on the left of the church entrance for the neat grave of Mr and Mrs Tiller. In the days of the 1950s and 1960s this couple had a famous troupe of dancing girls.

3 Turn left along the narrow alley from the church to the minor road in **Glasson**. Cross the road and turn right onto the new footpath. Return over the viaduct to the **Conder Green** car park.

Places of interest nearby

Cockersand Abbey was built by Premonstratensian monks in 1190 and the remnants are reached by a well-marked footpath from Glasson. The dissolution in 1537 and the ravages of the sea have destroyed all except the splendid old Chapter House where the monks carried out their business affairs.

For the energetic, a 4-mile linear walk along the old railway track from Conder Green leads to **St George's Quay** in the heart of old Lancaster. Here is the old Customs House, designed by a member of the old Gillow family, which is now a splendid maritime museum. ☎ *01524 64637* for opening times.

5 **Hornby**

The Royal Oak

This varied walk has everything, from quiet roads overlooking ancient historical sites to lush green meadows and a castle nearby. The riverside sections of the route afford panoramic views over open countryside and are spanned by famous bridges. There are places to picnic or just to stop and stare at the wide variety of wildlife. A camera and a pair of binoculars will add even more to this walk, which is an exciting exploration and a fascinating tale of two rivers.

Lancashire

THE PUB *'There is nothing which has been contrived by man by which so much happiness is produced as by a good tavern or inn.'* These wise words written by Dr Johnson in 1776 can be read at the entrance to the **Royal Oak**, located on the A683 through Hornby, the old coaching road between Kirkby Lonsdale and Lancaster. The inside is unspoiled and the menu is both varied and substantial, with children and vegetarians well looked after. On Monday and Wednesday evenings traditional fish and chips are on the menu and Thursday is designated as Steak Night. There is always an imaginative blend of international and traditional dishes, and soup and a variety of sandwiches are also on offer. Walkers are welcome. At the rear is a sheltered garden area ideal for family groups and pets. The choice of coffees is wide and I always look forward either to the soup of the day or the jacket potatoes.

☎ *01524 221228*

Distance 3 miles.

OS OL 2 Yorkshire Dales - Southern & Western areas and **OL** 41 Forest of Bowland & Ribblesdale. GR 586683.

Road walking for a short distance but good stretches of woodland and riverside scenery. One short section can be muddy after rain.

Starting Point The car park in the centre of Hornby.

How to get there Hornby lies on the A683 north-east of Lancaster. There is free parking close to the bridge over the River Wenning.

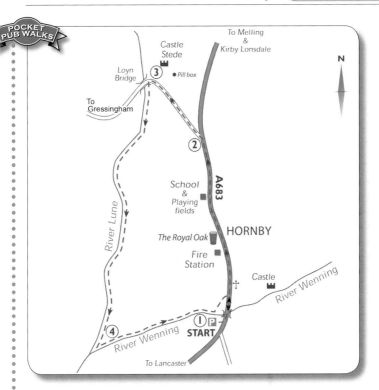

POCKET
PUB WALKS

To Melling
&
Kirby Lonsdale

Castle
Stede

Loyn
Bridge

(3)

• Pill box

N

To
Gressingham

(2)

A683

School
&
Playing
fields

River Lune

HORNBY

The Royal Oak

Fire
Station

Castle

River Wenning

(4)

River Wenning

START

To Lancaster

1 From the car park turn left and cross the bridge over the **River Wenning**.

Look up to the right and see the privately-owned Hornby Castle. The site was occupied by the Montbegons family as early as the 11th century. Parts of the present castle date to the 13th century but it has been added to and restored many times. The view from the bridge is very beautiful and was painted by Turner, the famous 18th-century artist. Continue along the road and to the right is the wonderful church of St Margaret of Antioch. This was built by Sir Edward Stanley who was one of the heroes of the battle of Flodden in 1514. Henry VIII rewarded Sir Edward for his part in defeating the Scots and made

Hornby Castle seen from the River Wenning.

him Lord Monteagle and gave him money. Some of this money was used to build the church tower. Here also is the remnant of an Anglo-Saxon cross which proves that the Hornby area was settled prior to the 8th century.

Continue along the road for less than ½ mile, passing the fire station, the **Royal Oak** and the school which are all on the left.

[2] As the A683 ascends gently, look out for a very minor road on the left leading to **Gressingham**. Turn left and keep on the left of the road. The fields on the left and right are a delight to all naturalists and this stretch should not be rushed. Follow the road for about ½ mile.

To the right look out for a Second World War pillbox. Above this concrete structure is a high point on which there was an ancient fortification. This was a motte (a fortified house) and a bailey (a courtyard) and was called **Castle Stede**. *It was the stronghold of the Montbegons before they moved their base to Hornby.*

3 Descend to **Loyn Bridge** and find a footpath to the right. Pass through a squeeze stile and descend towards the **River Lune**. Look for a set of stone steps. Descend these steps and turn left. Pass underneath the bridge. This was described as dilapidated in 1591 but there was probably a span there from the 14th century. Whilst passing under the bridge look out for the ancient ford. This was guarded in the old days by **Castle Stede** which overlooks the Lune. This stretch of the walk can be muddy after rain but from the ford the route ascends to a ladder stile. Cross this and pass through a deciduous woodland area, keeping the **River Lune** to the right. Follow the obvious riverside footpath which soon reaches the confluence of the **River Lune** with the **River Wenning**.

4 At this confluence turn sharp left and continue through woodland and alongside cottages, keeping the **Wenning** on the right. The final stretch is paved and reaches the village of **Hornby** close to the entrance to the castle opposite. Turn right and cross the bridge before returning to the **car park** starting point.

Places of interest nearby

> **Kirkby Lonsdale**, north on the A683, is a splendid little market town on the Cumbrian border and has excellent shopping, wonderful views of the River Lune and an impressive Norman church.
>
> In the other direction, the city of **Lancaster** is close by with its Roman remains, one of the finest Norman castles in England, a medieval church and a Victorian shopping centre.

Redirected path
Does not go down to river

Bolton-by-Bowland

The Coach & Horses

A stroll with a silver lining, this should not be either missed or rushed. It follows a section of the River Ribble and passes close to some of its minor tributaries, with areas of splendid woodland. Bolton-by-Bowland is a fine example of an old English village with its pub and nearby parish church, which is one of Lancashire's most ancient structures. Here are royal connections dating back to the 15th century, ancient trees, the ruins of a majestic old hall, another hall (which stinks!) and unspoiled riverside walks. All that glistens may not be gold but there is a silver connection here, which goes back to the time of Elizabeth I.

Distance 3 miles

OS OL 41 Forest of Bowland and Ribblesdale. GR 788495.

A gentle stroll on minor roads and riverside paths.

Starting Point The Coach & Horses at Bolton-by-Bowland.

How to get there Bolton-by-Bowland is to the north of the A59 between Sawley and Gisburn. From the Sawley turn-off, pass the ruins of the small Cistercian abbey to the right. Turn left at the Spread Eagle and then right over the bridge spanning the Ribble. Just beyond the bridge a right turn indicates Bolton-by-Bowland. At the Copy Nook Inn turn sharp right into the village. There is parking around the village lanes and close to the Coach & Horses and the smaller of the two greens.

THE PUB

The Coach & Horses is now a quiet and well-appointed country pub but this was not always the case. Before modern roads were built to accommodate the increasing numbers of fast-moving cars, inns such as the Coach & Horses were vital to the efficient operation of the turnpike system. This excellent little hostelry has retained all of its traditions and yet still caters well for modern travellers who may arrive by car or on foot. Good substantial sandwiches, tea and coffee are on offer but the grills and Sunday lunches are popular features. It has a cosy and welcoming feel and the menu, wine list and beers have been well planned. Please note that no food is available all day Tuesday.

☎ *01200 447202*

1 The walk begins by the **Coach & Horses** and the smaller of the two village greens.

This is dominated by a set of stocks set close to stone steps that once served as the market cross and as a whipping post. The place is much more peaceful these days but Bolton-by-Bowland dates back to before the Norman Conquest, when it was called Bodetun, which means 'the bow by the river', a good description of the meandering Ribble.

Follow the road out of the village towards **Gisburn** and in 200 yards reach the church of **St Peter and St Paul** on the left.

In 1468 Sir Ralph Pudsay restored the Norman church and this is thought to have been influenced by Henry VI, who was hidden by the Pudsays following the king's defeat at the battle of Hexham in 1464.

The Norman church at Bolton-by-Bowland.

POCKET
PUB WALKS

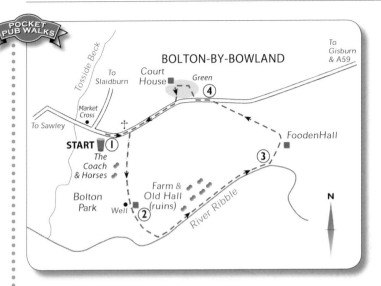

Inside the church is a memorial to Sir Ralph himself. Here was a fertile knight who had 25 children by three wives – no wonder the memorial is a large one because each individual is commemorated!

Opposite the church is an iron gate and a footpath leading to what is left of Sir Ralph's manor house, **Bolton Hall**. It was once described as the finest half-timbered house in Lancashire but it was sadly demolished in the 1960s. Follow the wide track through **Bolton Park,** which is lined by ancient trees.

2 Pass the ruins of **Bolton Hall** and bear right to **King Henry's Well**.

This was a bathhouse erected over a pure spring and was a favourite bathing place for the king in hiding.

Follow the footpath until it meets the **River Ribble** and then turn left along the path.

William Pudsay is said to have had a private but illicit silver mine in the area and minted his own coins. When pursued by customs officials he escaped over the cliffs and crossed the Ribble and set off to

London to seek pardon from Queen Elizabeth I. This was granted for two reasons. Firstly, he was her godson, but even more importantly, he gave her his silver mine!

3. After 400 yards, bear left away from the river and approach **Fooden Hall farm**.

This was once a small Tudor hall but is now a farmhouse. A stream runs through the grounds, which stinks of hydrogen sulphide. The water was once drunk by visitors who paid well for its healing properties, including a cure for infertility. Perhaps Sir Ralph himself drank lots of this water!

At **Fooden** turn sharp left along an obvious footpath and in less than ½ mile reach the **Gisburn** to **Bolton-by-Bowland** road.

4. Turn left along the road and reach the larger of the two village greens on the right. This is lined with ancient buildings including the **Old Courthouse** which dates to the 15th century. It has a weather vane on the roof depicting a fox. After exploring the green descend back to the starting point, passing the **church** on the right.

Places of interest nearby

Clitheroe, along the A59 to the south-west, is a delightful small market town with a well-preserved Norman castle, part of which serves as a museum depicting life in the Ribble Valley.
☎ *01200 424635/424568*

Whalley Abbey is a Cistercian monastery dating back to the 14th century. There is a visitor centre, with exhibitions, and a tea room in the grounds.
☎ *01254 822268*

7 Downham & Twiston

The Assheton Arms

This walk is a joy, not only for the beautiful scenery but also for its historic and wildlife interest. It follows narrow winding roads, crosses tumbling streams close to an old corn mill, and flirts with splendid belts of woodland. Look around and you enjoy the natural world, but look up and you have superb views of the foothills of Pendle. This stroll ensures that its scenery is ever-changing from 'mist over Pendle' to the sweep of Downham and Twiston in glorious sunshine.

THE PUB The **Assheton Arms** was formerly known as the George and Dragon but the name of the family long resident at Downham Hall has been adopted. Television viewers, however, may know it as the Signalman's Arms in the successful series *Born*

Distance 5 miles.

OS OL 41 Forest of Bowland and Ribblesdale. GR 783444.

Easy walking. Some muddy areas but they present no problem if suitable footwear is worn.

Starting Point The Downham village car park.

How to get there From the A59 linking Clitheroe with Gisburn turn off to the west to Chatburn. In the village, look for a sign indicating Downham and take this minor road back over the A59. Pass Downham's St Leonard's church on the right and descend the village street. Cross a bridge over a stream to reach the substantial free car park on the right.

and Bred. Once a farmhouse, the building dates back to 1765. The 'Ash', as it is affectionately known, has long catered for visitors, with a variety of beers on offer, as well as a comprehensive menu. The seafood has become famous and recipes using the local beef and mutton are also features of the pub. Tea and coffee are on offer and in the summer there are tables outside facing the ancient stocks and with Pendle as an attractive backdrop. There is a cosy interior with beams, small rooms and furniture with a feel of a bygone but luxurious time. Children and dogs are welcome.

☎ *01200 441227*

1 From the car park bear left to the bridge over **Downham Beck**. Turn left over the bridge and pause to enjoy the sight of mallards begging for food and the occasional dipper and grey wagtail which breed on the river and ignore the visitors. Ascend between

old cottages which became the film set for the TV series *Born and Bred*. Pass the old **school** on the right.

This street and the local countryside was also the setting for the 1960s classic black and white film Whistle Down the Wind *starring Hayley Mills.*

2 Almost at the top of the hill find **St Leonard's church** to the left and the **Assheton Arms** to the right.

Parts of the church date back to Norman times. In the 15th-century tower hang three bells which once called the monks of Whalley Abbey to prayer and inside is a font given to John Paslew, this Cistercian monastery's last abbot. He was executed on the orders of Henry VIII for the part he played in a rebellion known as the Pilgrimage of Grace in 1536.

Turn right at the church and pass the **Assheton Arms** and the **post office** on the left. Follow a very narrow road for about 1 mile. This twists and turns before descending into a lush valley with a stream running through it.

3 The road leads into the tiny hamlet of **Twiston**.

This can now be described as a naturalist's paradise but there is also a great deal to interest the historian. Running through the hamlet is

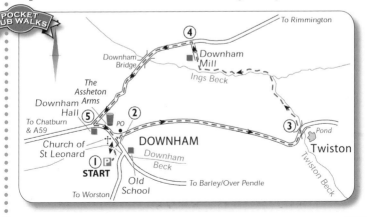

The remains of Twiston Mill.

Ings Beck, which is 'nobbut' a little stream these days. Before the Norman Conquest, however, Ings Beck was the boundary between the ancient Anglo-Saxon kingdoms of Mercia and Northumbria. The old spelling of Twiston was Twyssulton, which simply means a settlement on a boundary. Little remains but there are signs of an old mill and its pond is a haven for wildlife including moorhen, coot, heron and several species of dragonfly – the monks of Whalley had a corn mill at Twiston in 1327, which was powered by the beck.

Pass the old **mill pond** on the right and descend towards a barn. Turn left through a narrow squeeze stile and follow **Ings Beck**. Follow the track over several stiles and footbridges across the beck with an attractive mixed (mainly conifer) wood on the left. The wildlife around the beck is all that one could hope for, with one unexpected surprise. There are regular sightings of resident kingfishers, grey wagtails and dippers plus a most unusual avian visitor. This is the Mandarin duck, which is a colourful Asian species that has escaped from collections and is now breeding successfully in a few parts of Britain.

Continue to follow the obvious footpath to reach **Downham**

Mill in approximately ½ mile. The limits of the old mill pond (locally called lodges) and the leet leading to the long-gone waterwheel can still be identified. The 17th-century mill is now a private residence but the footpath passes the building on the right. Go ahead along a wide drive and in less than 200 yards reach a road.

4. **Rimington** is indicated right, but turn left and continue along the road towards **Downham**.

5. This reaches the minor road to **Chatburn** and straight ahead is the magnificent **Downham Hall.**

The manor once belonged to a Saxon named Aufrey but after the Conquest, William gave Downham to the de Lacys. In 1558 Roger Assheton bought the estate and it has been under that family's control ever since. The elder male member of the family has the title of Lord Clitheroe.

At the road junction turn left and find an old Roman gravestone close by. Bear right at the church on the right and the **Assheton Arms** on the left. Look straight ahead for a magnificent view of **Pendle**. Descend the main street and almost opposite the **Old School** turn right along a narrow lane which leads back to the car park.

Places of interest nearby

Gisburn has a Thursday cattle market and a well-preserved Norman church. Here is the grave of Francis Duckworth. He wrote the hymn tune *Rimington* to celebrate his birth in the nearby village of that name. He also wrote other less well known tunes called *Gisburn* and *Downham*.

The **Black Bull Hotel** in **Rimington** has its own transport museum, with steam locomotive and trans Atlantic liner memorabilia.
☎ *01200 445220*

The Pendle Inn

This stroll ascends gently towards Pendle, which is seen towering above attractive reservoirs. The route then goes through 'Witch Country' to the village of Roughlee and returns to Barley along a delightful riverside path. Here, with kingfishers and dippers for company, the walker can literally find an old mill by the stream. What more could be asked for? This is a glorious mix of history and natural history.

THE PUB
Although only built in 1930 the **Pendle Inn** in Barley is a comfortable pub that has recently extended its dining facilities to include an excellent restaurant. The choice of beers is good and the bar snacks varied and substantial. The Pendle, as its name implies, is overlooked by the hill with its traditions

of witchcraft and is often swept by winds. The 'evil atmosphere', however, is mostly a figment of fiction whilst the facts reveal glorious views, winding paths and rich natural history. Walkers are welcome here for a pint whilst those who have to drive will find tea and coffee on offer all day.

☎ *01282 614808*

1. From the car park head towards **Pendle**, passing through a picnic site and keeping a fast-running little stream on the left. Cross a wooden footbridge opposite the **Pendle Inn** and turn right along the road. Continue through the children's playground and past the **Barley Mow** restaurant on the right. Walk through the village, with a teashop and the Methodist chapel on the right.

Distance 5 miles.

OS OL 21 South Pennines, and **OL** 41 Forest of Bowland and Ribblesdale. GR 825404.

Following pleasant and undulating footpaths beside reservoirs and rivers and overlooked by Pendle Hill. There is a stretch along quiet roads.

Starting Point Barley car park.

How to get there *Barley is about 3 miles west of Nelson. From the A682 through Nelson, at the White Bear pub in Barrowford, turn left to Roughlee. At the Bay Horse in Roughlee turn left and follow the signs to Barley. The village is reached from Preston and Clitheroe via the A59 through Downham and over Pendle Hill. Barley car park is pay-and-display, with toilets, an information centre and picnic area.*

2 As the road sweeps left, a footpath sign indicates **Black Moss reservoir** and **Blacko** to the right. Follow the obvious track which ascends to reach **Upper Black Moss reservoir** on the left.

Completed in 1852 to supply water for the developing cotton town of Nelson, this has a capacity of around one million gallons (4.5 million litres) and has proved very attractive to wildfowl.

Continue along the very obvious track which sweeps gently left and then sharply right. Look for **Aitken Wood** on the right, which is the haunt of heron and sparrowhawk.

To the left is Lower Black Moss reservoir built in 1865 to provide Nelson with a further half million gallons of essential water. To the left

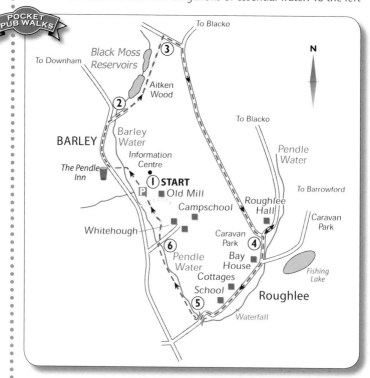

Looking towards Pendle Hill.

of both reservoirs are splendid views of Pendle.

The track then sweeps left, passing a stream on the right.

[3] When the track meets a narrow road, turn right and follow this winding undulating road, turning right at the T-junction to descend steeply into **Roughlee** after ¾ mile. Pass a caravan site on the right and then walk between rows of neat old cottages dating to the 17th and 18th centuries.

[4] Divert left for a few yards to view **Roughlee Hall**, now hemmed in by houses but here was the Tudor home of Alice Nutter who was executed as one of the Pendle Witches in 1612. Retrace your steps and pass through **Roughlee** village. Pass a waterfall, which was actually a steep weir built to provide water for an early 19th-century cotton mill. Follow the road past the school and approach a narrow bridge.

5 At the bridge a footpath is indicated right. Keep the stream called **Pendle Water** on the right and pass **Thorneyholme Farm** (another former cotton mill) on the left. Continue through fields and cross a couple of narrow stiles. To the left is a marshy area which is the only remnant of the old mill lodge.

6 At another stile meet a very narrow road at **Whitehough**. Turn right and then immediately left and continue to follow **Pendle Water** but this time the stream is on the left. Follow the very pretty track for about ½ mile to reach the delightful little hamlet of **Narrowgates**.

'Gate' is the Scandinavian word for a track and at this point it is indeed narrow. Narrowgates in the early 19th century had a cotton mill with associated cottages built for the workers. The mill and the cottages are now privately owned and have been beautifully restored.

From **Narrowgates** an obvious woodland path leads back to the car park in **Barley** after about 200 yards.

Places of interest nearby

The village of **Newchurch-on-Pendle** is just to the south of Barley, with its associations with the activities of the Pendle Witches who were executed at Lancaster in 1612. It is believed that Alice Nutter, the main character in the witches saga is buried in St Mary's churchyard in Newchurch and her resting place is marked.

The **Pendle Heritage Centre** at Barrowford has a café, a book shop and a museum covering the detailed history of the region. ☎ *01282 661702.*

Take walking poles - May be muddy in places.

The Strawbury Duck

This pleasant stroll has everything that an energetic family could hope for. It passes alongside large reservoirs, which have become popular with birdwatchers, and then through stretches of mixed woodland. There are reminders of the once dominant textile history and the chance to visit one of Lancashire's most famous pubs, all overlooked by the sweeping foothills of the West Pennines. Birds of prey such as the short-eared owl and merlin often add interest to the walk, and ravens and peregrine falcons are also sometimes seen.

THE PUB The **Strawbury Duck**, situated along a cul-de-sac opposite the railway station at Entwistle, is an inn of character with 18th-century beams, small cosy rooms and an excellent cuisine. There are plenty of local flavours with Bury black pudding, Entwistle hotpot, Entwistle trout and also locally reared Goosnargh Strawbury Duck. The lamb rack of ribs and home-made soups attract lots of custom. There are pleasant outdoor garden areas and an extensive car park which the pub shares with the station. The spelling of Strawbury comes as a surprise to most visitors.

☎ *01204 852013*

1. From the car park and picnic site turn right onto the embankment of the **Turton and Entwistle reservoir**.

    This was built in 1838 to produce a reliable water supply for a bleach works in the Bradshaw Valley situated below. In 1863 the reservoir was adapted to provide drinking water needed by the developing town of Bolton.

    Follow the path along the reservoir dam and pass a water tower on the left and a cottage on the right. Follow **Overshores Road** (which is not suitable for motor traffic) and ascend to the railway

---

Distance 3 miles. *4 miles*

OS Explorer 287 West Pennine Moors. GR 723175.

An undulating rather than challenging route, which has lots of quiet sheltered spots, with seats providing ideal picnic places and panoramic viewing areas.

Starting Point Batridge Lane car park.

How to get there *Follow the B6391 Green Arms road between Darwen and Chapeltown. Look for a sign on Batridge Lane indicating a free car park and picnic site, which is situated close to the Turton and Entwistle reservoir.*

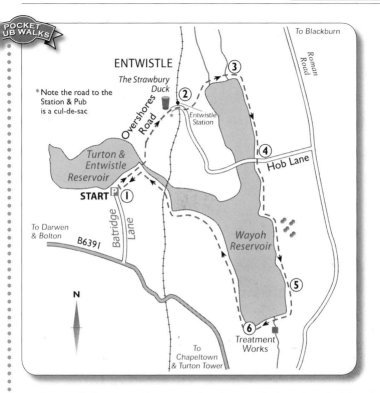

To Blackburn

Roman Road

ENTWISTLE

The Strawbury Duck ②

③

* Note the road to the Station & Pub is a cul-de-sac

Overshores Road

Entwistle Station

④

Hob Lane

Turton & Entwistle Reservoir

START P ①

Batridge Lane

To Darwen & Bolton

B6391

Wayoh Reservoir

⑤

⑥

Treatment Works

N

To Chapeltown & Turton Tower

station and the **Strawbury Duck**. The word 'bury' probably indicates the site of a fortification, which may date to the Roman period or perhaps earlier.

② At the railway, cross over a bridge and look out for a substantial stile on the left. Cross a field and descend to a woodland.

An iron gantry crosses the footpath and this once supported a long vanished pulley system. In Victorian times this carried goods from a bleach mill to the station. The Know Mill Works was in operation until 1958 when it was dismantled to make room for a substantial enlargement of the Wayoh reservoir.

Wayoh Reservoir.

Cross two footbridges over feeder streams to the **Wayoh reservoir**.

3 Turn sharp right and keep the reservoir on the right.

This is the place to enjoy the wide variety of birds, including resident great crested grebes.

4 Cross over Hob Lane and continue to follow the obvious reservoir path.

Hob Lane was once on the route of the Roman road called Watling Street and was an important link between Manchester and the equally important fort at Ribchester. 'Chester' simply means a fortification. This whole area is a haven for naturalists, with botanists delighting in the plants, whilst in the winter the birdlife is famous for its numbers and variety. There is now a resident flock of Canada geese which divides its time between the two reservoirs. The geese use the water for roosting and feed on grass on the verges.

5 Almost at the end of **Wayoh reservoir** there is a splendid viewpoint.

Wayoh was built in 1876 and its construction was also stimulated by the building of several bleach works in the Bradshaw Valley below. There was a massive extension to the reservoir in 1962 as Bolton demanded more and more drinking water. The views from this point are spectacular and include the steeple of St Anne's church at Chapeltown. There is also a good view of the railway viaduct built by the Blackburn, Darwen & Bolton Railway Company in 1848.

Just after this viewpoint turn right along the **Wayoh** embankment.

The modern water treatment works down to the left is capable of treating 10 million gallons (45 million litres) of water each day. Whilst United Utilities allow free access to the reservoirs, the treatment works are obviously kept private for safety reasons.

6 After the treatment works turn sharp right and follow the track alongside the reservoir. Follow it through stretches of mixed woodland and pass under the railway. The reservoir track continues to be easy to follow and returns you to the starting point and car park.

Places of interest nearby

Jumbles Country Park and Information Centre, to the south of Wayoh reservoir off the A676, has a very attractive little museum, coffee shop and a circular nature trail running round the reservoir which was built in the early 1970s.

☎ 01204 853360

At **Turton Tower Museum** the building is set around a medieval pele tower built as a defence against the invading Scots during the 14th century. Turton, between Jumbles and Wayoh, is now a splendid museum with lots of Civil War armour on display. There is a café, a bookshop and from the tower a network of footpaths lead out onto the moors. One route passes close to what remains of a stone circle showing that there were human settlements here long before written records began.

☎ 01204 852203

10 Roddlesworth

The Royal Arms

A **walk that makes the most** of Roddlesworth Woods, planted in 1904 by Liverpool Corporation to prevent erosion to the valley sides and thus protect the water supply. There are conifers here but also lots of native species, including oak, birch and some beech. The woods surround reservoirs, which attract waterbirds, while in the spring and summer the wild flowers are a joy, especially the carpets of succulent sweet-smelling bluebells. Open spaces afford panoramic views of open moorland and a number of pleasant little streams. These pass through the ruins of ancient farms and feed a healing well. There are places along the route to stop and stare at the wildlife and enjoy a quiet rest or to picnic in the sunshine.

Distance 4½ miles

OS Explorer 287 West Pennine Moors. GR 665215.

This is an undulating and at times steep stroll, which nevertheless has been adapted for wheelchair access. At the nearby Information Centre motorised wheelchairs can be hired but these do need to be booked in advance (☎ 01254 704502).

Starting Point The Roddlesworth Information Centre car park.

How to get there The Roddlesworth Nature Walks and Reservoirs are situated south of the historic village of Tockholes, signed off the A666 between Blackburn and Darwen and also from the A675 which links Bolton and Preston. The Information Centre, which has a café, is signed off the minor road south of Tockholes and shares a free car park with the Royal Arms.

THE PUB

The **Royal Arms** is a typical Victorian pub, from which there are spectacular views over the Darwen Moors dominated by the Jubilee Tower built to celebrate the Diamond Jubilee of Queen Victoria in 1897. The beer, soft drinks and hot beverages on offer take a lot of beating and the menu is to say the least impressive. The starters include mussels and smoked salmon and among the main courses are duck, lemon sole and lamb shank. There are good vegetarian options and the entire menu, including the sweets, varies according to seasonal availability. The whole place has retained its Victorian elegance and has a very welcoming atmosphere.

☎ 01254 705373

Lancashire

1 From the **Information Centre** cross the minor road and pass through a gate to the left. A footpath indicating the reservoirs leads off to the right. Follow this obvious and undulating path through trees for just over ½ mile.

The path leads to Upper Roddlesworth Reservoir, which was built as one of three by Liverpool Corporation between 1851 and 1864. They are still kept in perfect order by United Utilities. This is the place to enjoy the activities of the summer-visiting spotted flycatcher. Flycatchers have a unique method of feeding. They perch on a prominent branch. When they see an insect they fly after it, catch it and then return to the same location. No other species does this so continually or so elegantly.

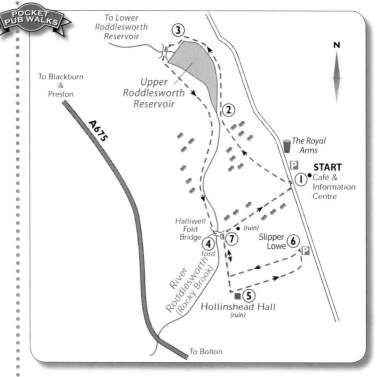

2 Follow the track around the reservoir, on which wildfowl winter and great crested grebes breed.

Halliwell Fold Bridge.

3 Bear left around the top of the reservoir and, at the end of this, cross a feeder stream via an attractive wooden bridge. This was brought all the way from Bideford in Devon but the translocation has been a success. There is fishing in the area with details available from the Information Centre. Bear left from the bridge and then right, keeping the **River Roddlesworth** (locally known as Rocky Brook) on the left.

4 Turn left over **Halliwell Fold Bridge** and then immediately right across a shallow ford onto **Mill Lane**. Until the reservoirs were built there was a mill powered by the river and a number of farms here. The ruins of these can still be seen. Follow **Mill Lane** and continue along this for around ¾ mile.

5 Follow the signs to **Hollinshead Hall**.

This was once the manor house for Tockholes but all that is visible today are the ruins of the 18th-century hall and the 19th-century farmhouse. The only structure still standing is the Georgian Well House built to cover over an ancient spring which was said to cure eye complaints and attracted pilgrims from at least Saxon times.

Follow an obvious track from the **Well House** to meet a minor road.

6 Walk along the road for approximately 400 yards and approach **Slipper Lowe** car park.

'Lowe' means a prehistoric burial ground and a Bronze Age spearhead has been found nearby. There is a steep hill hereabouts and the word 'slipper' relates to the shape of the brake shoes fitted to horse-drawn vehicles in the 18th century.

Turn left along a path from the car park and then right to return down **Mill Lane** to **Halliwell Fold Bridge**. Turn right at the bridge and follow the signs for the **Information Centre**.

7 Ascend the steep track through the woodlands, which are full of bluebells in the spring.

In medieval times bluebells were 'farmed' because the sticky sap in the stems was partially evaporated to produce a powerful glue. It is likely that a man named Fletcher used the glue to fasten the flights to the arrows carried by another artisan called Archer, whose weapon was produced by another craftsman called Bowman!

Return along the steep ascent to the **Information Centre** and the **Royal Arms**.

Places of interest nearby

The de Hoghtons first came to England with William the Conqueror and have been in residence at **Hoghton Tower** since the 14th century. The Tower, to the north-west and approached off the A675 west of Blackburn, is open to the public during the summer.
☎ *01254 852986*

Tockholes village is a quiet backwater and in the churchyard is the base of a 'tock' or touch stone which was a meeting place for Christians even before a Saxon church was built. Also in the grounds of the modern church is an outdoor pulpit, a reminder of the times when congregations were often so large that there was a spill-over into the churchyard.

The Duke of Wellington

This is a fascinating stroll to and around one of Lancashire's oldest reservoirs. The area shows the development of industrial Lancashire to perfection. The route leads to ruined halls, farmhouses and cottages which were once the home of illicit whiskey distillers. Lancashire whiskey is still distilled in Wigan but the Haslingden Grane variety has long gone. Here, too, are the remains of pleasure gardens and magnificent moorland scenery rich in industrial archaeology and natural history.

Lancashire

Distance 3 miles.

OS Explorer 287 West Pennine Moors. GR 767228.

The walk is level and is the haunt of rare breeding birds, including merlin and short-eared owl.

Starting Point The Duke of Wellington in Haslingden Grane.

How to get there Haslingden Grane is situated on the A6177 west of Haslingden. There is a very large car park at the Duke of Wellington; walkers should ask at the bar for permission to park. There is also free parking at the Clough Head Information Centre and café just beyond the pub.

THE PUB The **Duke of Wellington** is a Brewers Fayre house that has splendid views over the reservoir from the lounge and the large rear and secluded garden. Built following Wellington's victory at Waterloo in 1815, it once welcomed coach travellers during the turnpike period. Although now mainly open-plan, the outline of the old rooms can be seen by sitting in secluded corners and looking at the beams. The choice of beers and wines is wide and the menu is equally comprehensive. The Sunday roast beef is served in medium portions (which are large) and jumbo size which will defeat all but the most robust diners. The slow-cooked lamb is a treat as is the liver and bacon. Vegetarians and children are well looked after and the starters and sweets are varied and appetising.

☎ *01706 215610*

Haslingden Grane Walk 11

1 From the **Duke of Wellington** turn left along the A6177 for less than 200 yards and find **Heap Clough** on the right. Turn right to walk along **Heap Clough Road** to a cattle grid. Turn right to **Jacky Barn Farm**. Cross a wooden stile and follow an obvious fence to a wall. Pass through a gap and reach the ruins of **Leys End** and the remains of an old quarry. Cross a stone stile and into a planted area dominated by rhododendrons.

2 After ½ mile, approach the site of **Kettlewell Hall**. The gardens and its hall enjoyed a period of prosperity from 1916 to 1941 when the **Grane Tea Gardens** attracted large crowds. The area is still popular with picnickers who these days have to 'bring their own'. From the old gardens climb a wooden stile and descend along a sunken track to **Holden Hall**, now a hotel.

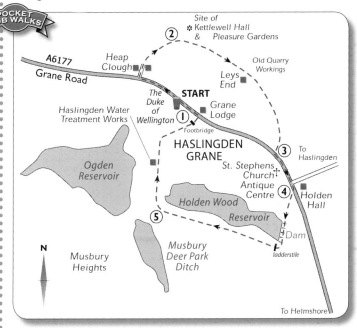

POCKET
PUB WALKS

Site of
✿ Kettlewell Hall
2 & Pleasure Gardens

A6177
Grane Road

Heap
Clough

Old Quarry
Workings

Leys
End

The
Duke
of
Wellington

START

Grane
Lodge

Haslingden Water
Treatment Works

1

Footbridge

**HASLINGDEN
GRANE**

St. Stephens
Church
Antique
Centre 4

3 To
Haslingden

Holden
Hall

Ogden
Reservoir

Holden Wood
Reservoir

5

Dam

N

Musbury
Heights

Musbury
Deer Park
Ditch

ladderstile

To Helmshore

The Clough Head Information Centre.

3 Approach a wall surrounding the cemetery. Turn left towards **Holden Hall** and walk towards **St Stephen's church** which is no longer used for services but is a popular antiques centre.

The Holden family first resided on the site from 1272 but their last hall was demolished in the 1890s. The ruins still have a nostalgic feel to them. St Stephen's church was built in the 1860s at a time when Haslingden Grane was prosperous. Following reservoir construction the church was demolished and rebuilt stone by stone on its present site. The local folk used to soak up much more than a religious spirit. Lancashire whiskey was brewed and exported illegally in large volumes and the question 'Do you want a brew?' meant alcohol and not tea! These days Lancashire whiskey has to be spelled with an 'e' to satisfy the Scots and the Trade Descriptions Act!

At the hall and church (antiques centre), you will see a footpath sign to the left.

4 Turn left along **Grane Road** (A6177) for a few yards and look for a lane on the right. Follow the footpath sign to **Holden Wood Reservoir**.

This was completed during the 1840s. It is now maintained by United Utilities and beneath the water are the remains of several farms. Those brewing whiskey hereabouts were then literally obliged to take a lot more water with it!

Cross the reservoir dam and bear right to a ladder stile. Look right and find a second ladder stile. Turn right and follow a fence across a damp area.

This area was once owned by Henry de Lacy, who in 1304 built a huge deer park and although this was abandoned in 1507 the outline can still be clearly seen.

5 Follow the well marked path for about ½ mile to a disused quarry. Turn right over an obvious stile and turn sharp left. Descend to the water treatment works with **Ogden Reservoir** on the left. Cross a footbridge, with **Grane Lodge** over on the opposite side of the A6177. Turn left along this road for a short distance back to the **Duke of Wellington**.

Places of interest nearby

Following a major refurbishment in 2007, **Helmshore Textile Museum**, about 1½ miles from the start of the walk, is now a world famous museum. Inside are working exhibits of woollen and cotton mills and the only working Arkwright Water Frame in the world. ☎ *01706 226459*

The **Clough Head Information Centre and Café**, situated to the right on the Blackburn side of Grane Road (the A6177), just beyond the Duke of Wellington pub, is a pleasant place for a picnic and there is also a small bookshop there. ☎ *01706 830162.*

12 **Worsthorne &**
Hurstwood

The Crooked Billet

This is an undulating stroll across lush fields and through woodland to a spacious reservoir, with many opportunities to enjoy the local birdlife, and includes a visit to two of Lancashire's most historic villages. Worsthorne has a mix of 16th-century cottages and millworkers' houses, while in the hamlet of Hurstwood are ancient cottages, stables and a fascinating old hall. This is also the place to explore the early life of one of England's most famous Tudor poets.

THE PUB

The **Crooked Billet** in Worsthorne is one of the finest village pubs in Lancashire and its 19th-century decor has been splendidly preserved. You can sit outside on a fine day and the menu is mouth-watering. The choice of beers is wide but tea, coffee and sandwiches are always on offer. More substantial items on the menu include meat produced locally and the Sunday roasts are popular. Those who wish to enjoy the succulent sweets should not start with the substantial soup of the day, which is a meal in itself!

☎ 01282 429040

Distance 3 miles.

OS OL 21 South Pennines. GR 876325.

Gentle ascents give sweeping views across hauntingly beautiful countryside.

Starting Point St John's church, Worsthorne.

How to get there *From Burnley, follow the Todmorden road (A646) and turn off to the north, signed Hurstwood and Worsthorne. Cross Salterford Bridge and on to Worsthorne. There is plenty of street parking in the village.*

1 The walk starts at **St John's church**.

This was built in the early 19th century but looks much older. It is unusual in that the local Thursby family who funded the building actually incorporated a bar within the church – here was literally a touch of the Christian spirit! Surrounding the church is some impressive ironwork which those interested in the craft of the blacksmith travel miles to appreciate.

Near the church and the **Bay Horse** pub, the second impressive hostelry in the village, is a footpath sign. Turn right past a row of cottages and follow the footpath down through lush fields.

2 After about ½ mile, the winding field path leads to a minor road, where you turn left to **Hurstwood**. Follow the road into

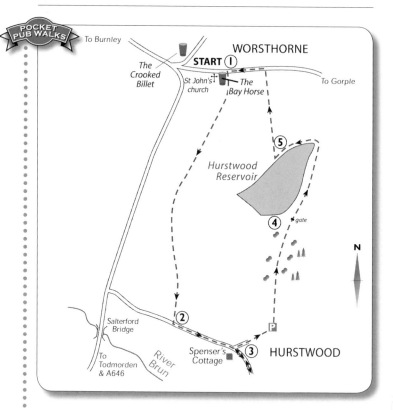

POCKET PUB WALKS

To Burnley

WORSTHORNE

The Crooked Billet

START ①

St John's church

The Bay Horse

To Gorple

⑤

Hurstwood Reservoir

④ ← gate

N

②

Salterford Bridge

To Todmorden & A646

River Brun

Spenser's Cottage

③ HURSTWOOD

Hurstwood and explore the village.

The privately-owned Hurstwood Hall dates to the 16th century. On the right is Spenser's Cottage. It is said that as a youth Edmund Spenser (1552-1599) lived in this cottage and fell in love with Rose Dyneley and wrote the Faerie Queen for her. His suit was rejected and Spenser went to London and dedicated the work to a joyous Queen Elizabeth I. The rest, as they say, is history! Spenser also wrote the Shepherd's Kalender which is written in a very recognisable Lancashire dialect. A few yards from the poet's cottage is a stable block still in use and known as Tattersall's Tenement. Richard Tattersall was *an excellent horseman who went off to London to seek his fortune. In 1766 he set up his horse sales in Knightsbridge. It is fascinating to see that these two famous figures lived within 50 yards of each other, even if in different centuries.*

Retrace the short road through the hamlet.

3 Turn right to reach a large car park. Follow the path through the mixed but mainly conifer woodlands to reach a substantial gate in around ½ mile. This area is a perfect breeding ground for the resident tawny owls.

4 Pass through the gate and follow the track, keeping **Hurstwood Reservoir** on the left.

The reservoir, completed in the 1920s, is overlooked by what are known as the hushings. This relates to the sound made by releasing water from large ponds. The current washed away the shallow soil to enable lead to be mined from the exposed outcrops of limestone. The hushings today look as if they have been eroded by a tidal wave.

At the end of the reservoir the path sweeps left.

5 After about 500 yards a footpath is indicated to the right. Follow this through a very pleasant area of fields and woodland to reach the substantial trackway between **Gorple** and **Worsthorne**. Turn left to return to the starting point of the walk in **Worsthorne**.

Places of interest nearby

About one mile from Worsthorne is 15th-century **Towneley Hall** which now houses a museum and art gallery. It is open daily except Saturday, free of charge. There are associated nature trails open at all times and wonderful woodland walks in the surrounding parkland.
☎ *01282 424213*

13 **Blackstone Edge**

The White House

Anyone who enjoys wild, spectacular countryside and a rich pattern of wildlife will love the ups and downs of this walk. From the cool woodland glades beside Hollingworth Lake, filled with bird song, to the upland heather and bracken-coloured slopes, the scene here changes by the minute, the day and the season. There are plenty of places to rest and enjoy this route, which passes along the Pennine and Rochdale Way footpaths, old packhorse routes, and what may well be one of the best preserved Roman roads in Britain. On clear days you can 'almost if not quite see for ever', and walking in the footsteps of the Roman legions adds an extra dimension of pleasure and interest.

Distance 6 miles.

OS OL 21 South Pennines. GR 941154.

A steep climb towards the summit but the return is all downhill. Sensible footwear should be worn, especially in wet weather when the steep and uneven route can become slippery.

Starting Point The Visitor Centre at Hollingworth Lake.

How to get there *Hollingworth Lake is well signed from the A58, between Rochdale and Halifax. At the traffic lights in Littleborough follow the B6225 which runs alongside the Rochdale Canal. At the edge of the lake turn left and then left again to the Visitor Centre and the very large pay and display car park.*

THE PUB Situated at the halfway point of this walk, the **White House** stands like a landmark high on the Pennines and is a welcome stop for walkers following the Pennine Way. It is an old coaching inn (originally called the Coach and Horses) dating from 1671 and is 1,300 feet above sea level. The hostelry, with its quaint alcoves and blackened beams, is rightly famous for its hand-pumped beers, especially the Theakston's bitter, first brewed in the early years of the 19th century. The menu is wide and the children's choice is much more healthy than most. The fresh fish is just that and local choices include Barnsley chops, which will challenge even the largest appetites. It is possible to eat outside in a quiet corner. The White House has two large car parks of its own but there is also another large car park close by which is free of charge.

☎ *01706 378456*

The walk begins at the Visitor Centre and café situated at the edge of Hollingworth Lake. This was built in the early years of the 19th century to supply compensation water for the Rochdale Canal; 33 miles of canal and 92 locks linking Manchester and Sowerby Bridge used lots of water and Hollingworth's 116-acre lake provided it. The lake has also functioned like an inland sea port ever since and is now overlooked by the M62 motorway, seen away in the distance.

1 From the huge car park, take the well signed path away from the **Visitor Centre** and through swathes of mixed woodland.

2 The woodland leads out into an open stretch of countryside from which a clear track leads steeply uphill towards **Blackstone Edge**. The Romans had to cross this peak and their straight line route can easily be seen above. Pass a golf course on the right. There is

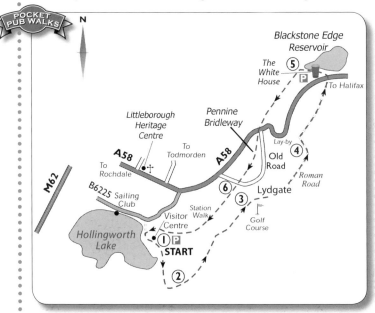

The delightful view from the Visitor Centre.

no confusing the path, which has been kept free of encroaching bracken by hundreds of eager feet.

3 At **Lydgate** you approach a minor road, but bear right away from this and follow the waymarked track of an ancient road.

The origins of this seem to have generated lots of heat but not a lot of light by serious historians. Does this track date to the Bronze Age, to the Romans or to the packhorses of medieval times up until the 19th century? The answer is probably all of these because what is the point of pioneering a new route when all you have to do is build on top of the old one?

Continue the steep climb along this old road to a stile.

4 Over the stile you come to a small layby, look around to enjoy the panoramic views and prepare for the last steep ascent which is just over ½ mile.

This route follows the line of an ancient drain and here you will meet Pennine Way walkers on their way to the White House for a meal and a well earned rest from carrying their backpacks. The White House and its stables will have been a relief for the coach horses because the climb up to the turnpike road (the modern A58) must have been exhausting. Above the hostelry there are still wide expanses of open moor but since the mid 19th century the Blackstone Edge reservoir has added variety to the scene and a pleasant footpath runs around it.

5 Enjoy your break at the **White House**. Resume the walk from the car park. Bear left and descend steeply to meet the A58 and a minor road. Cross the A58 and approach the minor road (once the old coach road). Keep this road on the left and follow the **Pennine Bridleway**.

6 At **Lydgate**, cross the old road and follow the steep descent along the obvious **Station Walk** back to the **Visitor Centre** and car park at **Hollingworth Lake**.

Places of interest nearby

Littleborough Coach House Visitor Centre is an excellent place to discover the history of the area and buy the relevant maps. The building in the centre of Littleborough, opposite the parish church, was an important base for coach travellers during the 18th and 19th centuries.
☎ *01706 378481*

Steanor Bottom Toll House is one of the best preserved toll houses in England and is privately owned. It is, however, easily seen on the left of the road between Littleborough and Todmorden. It is situated on the border between Lancashire and Yorkshire.

14 Springmill, Rochdale

The Bulls Head

Although this route passes close to four reservoirs, this is not a watery walk so much as a rural ramble or undulating stroll through unspoiled countryside with spectacular moorland views. Actually, it is a triumph of Mother Nature because this was once mining and cotton country but all traces of these industries have now gone. The presence of the reservoirs, fringed with mixed woodlands, has been a bonus for wildlife, and walkers who take their time will be rewarded by a bewildering variety of scenery, plants and wildlife.

Distance 3 miles.

OS Explorer 277 Manchester and Salford. GR 952124.

There are some steep but well maintained stretches, and easy descents.

Starting Point The large free car park at Ogden reservoir.

How to get there From the M62 turn off at Junction 21 and follow the A640 towards Newhey. Just before driving out of Newhey look for a sign to the left. This leads onto Ogden Lane and there is a sign advertising the Bulls Head, but continue ahead for about ¼ mile to the tiny hamlet of Springmill. Just before this there is a free car park and toilets at Ogden reservoir.

THE PUB The **Bulls Head** is a super little pub which attracts lots of customers even though it is situated in the very quiet hamlet of Ogden Lane. It is renowned for its cosy 19th-century atmosphere and its Sunday roasts. The menu is varied but don't miss the salads, the spare ribs starter or the home-made beef and steak and kidney puddings. If you have room for a sweet, the fruits in season are worth a visit on their own. There are also sandwiches, ideal for walkers who are made most welcome. Drinks include hand-pumped beers brewed by Thwaites of Blackburn, who have been in the business since 1807. There are picnic tables outside and a spacious car park. The pub is open every day except Monday.

☎ 01706 847992

From the car park you can see the retaining wall of Ogden reservoir and wooden steps leading up to it. Ogden was built in the 1870s and *provides drinking water for Oldham. Fishing takes place here and day tickets can be obtained from the warden's office near the toilet block or by ringing ☎ 01706 881049.*

1 To begin the walk, leave the car park to ascend the gentle slope through the lovely hamlet of **Springmill**, where there is a row of cottages built for those who worked at the Spring Mill. This was once a water-powered textile mill dating to the early years of the Industrial Revolution. After passing **Gate House**, which bears the datestone 1862, continue to ascend.

2 Follow the unsigned but obvious track to the left as it drops down towards **Kitcliffe Farm**. At a cattle grid turn through a gate, follow the footpath and keep close to the retaining wall of the reservoir

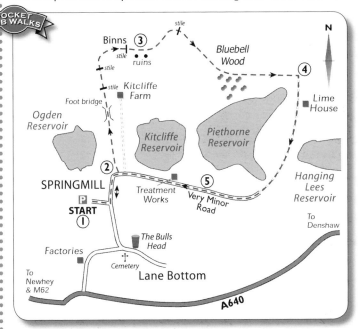

Springmill.

on the left. Descend steeply to a footbridge. Carry on and go over a series of four stiles which can clearly be seen leading up onto the moors. In about ½ mile, the path then sweeps right.

On the left are the ruins of a settlement dating back to the 13th century. Here were once barns, outbuildings, farmhouses and cottages. There are records to show that rye, barley, wheat and root crops, which were used to feed people and their livestock, were grown here. Oldham Corporation were allowed to acquire Binns by compulsory purchase in 1867 for the sum of £2,430 in order to construct their reservoirs.

3 The very clear footpath sweeps left and right before reaching **Old House Ground Plantation**, which locals refer to as the Bluebell Wood, on the northern side of **Piethorne reservoir**. United Utilities who now own the site allow the local wildlife trust to

look after the wood, which is a welcome contrast to the sweeping open moorlands.

4 At the end of **Piethorne reservoir** turn right where the footpath meets a wider track.

To the left is the old lime storehouse; this was shovelled into the feeder stream of the reservoir in order to reduce the natural acidity of the water. As modern treatment methods evolved the solidly constructed lime house became redundant.

5 The track sweeps right and as **Kitcliffe reservoir** is approached the modern treatment works can be seen down to the right. Today this treats 8 million gallons (nearly 35 million litres) of water each day. Descend into **Springmill** and back to the car park, and note that the toilet block and warden's office were once a weighbridge, not for textiles but for coal. All traces of mining have now vanished and this walk is set in the middle of idyllic countryside.

Places of interest nearby

Ellenroad Engine House nestles in the hills around Rochdale in the valley of the River Beal at Milnrow. It is almost at junction 21 off the M62 motorway. This is all that remains of one of the world's largest cotton spinning mills. The engine house and its machines have been fully restored and there is a bookshop and café.
☎ *01706 881952*

15 Ashurst Beacon

The Beacon Inn

Wonderful woodlands and wildlife, ancient history plus a climb to a beacon hill combine to provide one of the most beautiful strolls in the north-west of England. A winding footpath gives a steep climb at the start to the beacon and then descends more gently back to the pub and car park. The paths are popular with families and there are plenty of places to picnic and soak up the scenery. Naturalists will need to take time to explore the developing woodlands with the young oaks beginning to provide acorns, which are fed upon by birds such as jay and woodpigeon. At quiet times long-tailed field mice can be seen and in the warmer months there are good habitats for bats.

Distance 1½ miles

OS Explorer 285 Southport and Chorley. GR 502080.

A steep climb but a more gentle descent.

Starting Point The Ashurst Beacon car park.

How to get there *From the M6 turn off along the A5209 to Parbold. Pass through the village and turn left along Higher Lane which is a minor road. At Dalton church turn left onto Beacon Lane. After around 2 miles turn right into an extensive free car park surrounded by trees. From the Liverpool area the beacon can be reached from Skelmersdale and Up Holland.*

THE PUB Situated close to the Ashurst Beacon parking area, the **Beacon Inn** has its own extensive car park. The decor is reminiscent of a Victorian pub but the menu is both traditional and modern. As starters the soup and the breaded mushrooms are excellent and the grills are famous both for quantity and quality. Customers need to arrive early to enjoy the three course Sunday lunch. The 'Fish of the Day' dish is also worth travelling miles to enjoy. There is an extensive beer garden at the rear where pets and children are welcome. The sandwiches prove very popular with walkers.

☎ *01695 632323*

1 From the car park stroll to the minor road and turn left. Cross the road and after less than 50 yards find a stile. Cross the stile but note that although the footpath is obvious it is concessionary and is not signed. Ascend the wide track and pass through rows of oak and rowan trees. The **Ashurst Beacon** comes into view on an elevated site.

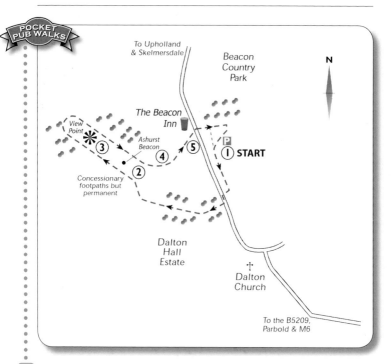

POCKET PUB WALKS

To Upholland & Skelmersdale

Beacon Country Park

N

The Beacon Inn

View Point

Ashurst Beacon

P

③ **④** **⑤** **①** **START**

②

Concessionary footpaths but permanent

Dalton Hall Estate

☩ Dalton Church

To the B5209, Parbold & M6

---

② Approach the Ashurst Beacon.

This straddles a ridge overlooking the fertile south Lancashire plain above the village of Parbold, through which passes the Leeds and Liverpool Canal. The beacon is surrounded by steps, which provide a delightful platform on which to soak up the views or enjoy a picnic. The prominent beacon has been part of the early warning system of invasion from medieval times but was a vital part in the chain of beacon hills as the Spanish Armada was approaching to threaten England. Who was Ashurst? The family lived in nearby Dalton at Ashurst Hall from the 15th century. Sir William decided in 1797 that Napoleon was a threat and replaced the existing beacon. The new structure was fitted with a cast-iron firebox which could be ignited at great speed. The position of these fire boxes can still clearly be seen.

Pass the beacon on the right and approach a concrete viewpoint.

The panorama from here is splendid and on a clear day you cannot see forever, but it does approach perfection. A viewfinder indicates that Great Orme is 47 miles away, Blackpool is 21, the Lake District 60 and the Bowland Fells 27. Manchester Airport is 24 miles away and Jodrell Bank can be seen at a distance of 29 miles.

3 A network of footpaths leads through woodlands dominated by oak and rowan. Sweep in a circle on the clear wide track around the woodlands and then pass the viewpoint and the **Ashurst Beacon** on the right.

Ashurst Beacon.

Lancashire

4 Just beyond a seat, the footpath diverges. Keep to the left and take time to explore the wildlife, which has resident goldfinches and stonechat. The footpath winds its way through trees and then descends steeply.

5 Approach a solid iron gate and cross the road. To the left and only 50 yards away is the **Beacon Inn**. After crossing the road pass through another substantial area of native woodland. The obvious path sweeps gently to the right and leads back into the car park.

Places of interest nearby

The delightful **Beacon Country Park** and golf course at Up Holland has a free car park and is run by the West Lancashire District Council. There are rolling meadows, quiet strolls and spacious picnic areas. There is a café and good toilet facilities. ☎ *01695 622794*

You can also take a stroll along the path surrounding the **Abbey Lakes** at Up Holland. This is an ideal place to watch birds. With the help of the Heritage Lottery fund, work is under way to trace the history of this area and make it more accessible. Details are available from Beacon Country Park at the phone number listed above.

Or visit the **Leeds and Liverpool Canal at Parbold**. Here in a conservation area is a barge marina dominated by the tower of a 19th-century windmill. The stroll along the towpath is a delight.